It Was Always Meant to Happen that Way.

Some things I have learned and taught as a life coach.

Brooke Castillo

ISBN: 978-0-9778539-6-0

Cover design: Cathi Stevenson

Page design: Janice Phelps Williams

www.janicephelps.com

PRINTED IN THE UNITED STATES OF AMERICA

To Diana and Kate
My favorite teachers of love and laughter

Table of Contents

"How do we know it was meant to happen that way?
"It did."
~Byron Katie

Preface

After I wrote my first book, I laid on the ground in complete exhaustion and told my husband to promise me he would never let me write another. It wasn't that the writing was so exhausting; it was the self-doubt that plagued me every day of the experience. It was something I had to overcome in order to write. When I wrote my second book, it was more of the same. I avoided it more, but it still pounded against my efforts as I wrote. And now, I willingly am entering into this process again. I am going into the fire in order to share what I must share, write what I must write and face my own demons yet again.

Books have saved my life and each time I read one that helps me in any way, I silently thank the author for having had the guts to write it. Most of them write much more intellectually and eloquently than I do, and yet I know they faced many of the same doubts I myself have faced. I feel as if their courage has weaved its way through their book and into my heart in order to make my life a bit better. And it has.

When I receive letters from my readers, I am amazed to find that my writing has done the same for them. I am overwhelmed by the gratitude so many people express to me in emails as they share how much my book has helped them. I feel very humbled and honored to be part of something that is beyond my own comprehension.

In this book, I hope I have the courage to be more of myself than I have ever been. I want to share with you all how much I struggle in my own life, with my own self coaching, and my own self doubt. I want you to know how hard I work on my own happiness and how much I think it is worth it.

I also want to share the things I have learned that have set me free from my own mind. I want to give you the simple tips that have transformed me and the deepest work that has given me permission to be the fullest expression of who I am.

I promise myself not to obsess about what you think of my writing. I am not going to try to please you. I am not going to try to impress you or show you that I am smart enough or worthy to be read. I am going to write what is in my heart and in my mind. This might have disastrous results and I am going to go there because you will be right there with me. We'll go together. I am going to ask you to come along for this ride into authenticity.

Authenticity is such a pretty word and it conjures images of beautiful women who look good without make-up. I am not one of those women. My authenticity is messy. It includes unshaven legs and frustration at my kids and too much time reading smutty magazines. But it is true. And so is everything I share in this book.

A lot of what you will read in this book was posted on my blog at one time or another. I pulled my own favorites and the ones that seemed to have the most impact on my readers. It's a collection of some of my most effective ideas, questions, thoughts and essays. I have received hundreds of emails of appreciation, and I think they bear repeating, especially the ones that I have retired from products I used to sell.

Since you have paid good money for this book, promise me one thing. You will do the book. Yes. Do it. Don't just read it and be entertained by it. Don't just mull it over. Get dirty. Answer the questions. Engage with it and with yourself. Come alive with it, don't just be a passenger along for the ride. Drive.

Blogging

I started writing a blog because that is what you are supposed to do when you are marketing your coaching business. I was nervous at first to press send when I was done, afraid that someone might judge me or that someone might figure out I don't know how to spell or where to put a comma. But what I was delighted to learn is that I don't have to follow any rules on my blog. I can put a period anywhere I. damn well please. And I do. I write how I want with my own rules and other people love to read it. Who knew life could be so amazing?

In this book I have included some of my favorite blog posts. You might have read them before. Reading them now, again, because you are in a different place might be useful or good. I have found that I can re-read a book when I am in a different place in my life and find something new.

Because I have already written a weight-loss book, I did not include most of the posts about weight and overeating. I did however include the ones that were universal to compulsive behavior of all kinds: drinking, shopping, smoking, etc.

To tell you the truth (because I promised I would), sometimes I read my own blog posts and learn something new. I am sometimes impressed that I wrote something that I have now forgotten and I can learn something as a student to my teacher. Sometimes I want to email myself and let me know that it helped. Indulgent? I guess so. Am I in love with myself? I guess, kinda. Unless I am thinking I am worthless and indulgent. But let's move on.

What I Do

So many people ask me what I do for a living even after I have told them. They want to know what the heck a life coach is. The truth is, I don't really know how to explain it without sounding arrogant at best or cheesy at worst. I usually avoid the question.

But since you have purchased this book, I will make my best effort to tell you what it is I do for a living.

***

I ask people great questions that help them get to know themselves.

I read amazing books and teach what I learn to my students.

I create new ideas based on a vast knowledge of self-help literature and share those ideas with my clients.

I tell my clients the truth: the truth that their friends won't tell them.

I help people see the downside of being mean to themselves.

I give people permission to be who they are.

I oppose any held belief that is not in my client's best interest.

I coach myself endlessly and then talk about what I have learned.

I excel at being a coach because my knowledge is deep and has been for a long time.

I understand my psyche and, therefore, usually can understand my clients'.

I show up when I want to quit.

I apologize when I want to yell.

I admit that I am fallible, infantile, and scared.

I ask my clients to reach for more of themselves.

I risk being unpopular by telling the truth.

I help people figure out why they do what they do so they can change it if they want to.

What I Believe

You are beautiful. Find it.

I can do whatever it is that feeds my soul and make a good living doing it.

My clients are brave.

Thoughts create our pain.

Byron Katie is amazing.

All homes should have lots of sunlight.

Money can teach you a tremendous amount about yourself.

People (all of us) just want you to think they are worthy, lovable, and fabulous.

Everyone should have a dog in order to learn about unconditional love.

Love is something we do, not something we feel.

Creation is our work.

We are all made for something. It is our job to be it, not just seek it.

When you know what you don't want, it gets you closer to what you do want.

Emotional maturity is difficult . . . and worth it.

Laughing matters a lot.

Everything can be a laughing matter.

Reading saved my life.

It's okay to say no.

We can't help anyone until we have helped ourselves.

The Universe has my back, yours too.

Everything that is meant to happen does.

Everything that isn't meant to happen doesn't.

Telling the truth is always freedom.

Pretending to be cool is exhausting.

Yelling hardly ever solves anything.

Simple is better than complicated.

Inspiration is created and earned, not given.

No one has it easy.

Appreciating matters.

Blame sucks.

Who I Coach

I coach the most amazingly brilliant women on the planet. I coach you. I coach women who are tired of being fat and tired of being in pain and tired of being married to the wrong guy or tired of their jobs.

I coach people who believe there is a better way to live your life than to be broke and find yourself drinking a bottle of wine every night.

I coach women who give to everyone but themselves in the hope that someone will approve of them and love them, everyone but themselves.

I coach people who think they are victims. (They aren't.) Being victimized and taking on the role of victim are different.

I coach clients who believe in God and those who think God is Santa Claus for adults.

I coach doctors, PhDs, Harvard/Princeton/MIT graduates and I coach clients who didn't finish high school. Their pain all hurts the same.

I coach people who don't even like me. They hire me to judge me.

I coach people who don't need coaching; they just want to borrow my coaching ideas. (Fine by me, by the way!)

I coach people desperate and in despair and holding on by a thread with only a glimmer of hope.

I coach people who have no hope, who can barely whisper into the phone.

I coach women who have been raped, molested, beaten, and abandoned.

I coach clients who make over one million dollars a year who aren't happy, and ones who make nothing who are.

I coach anyone who is willing to find a way to feel better.

I coach the readers of my books, the readers of my blog, my friends, my kids, my family, and strangers.

But most importantly, very most importantly, I coach myself, every damn day.

What Do I Want to Write?

I want to write a book I want to read. I love books that don't follow the rules and don't fill up every page. I loved reading The War of Art because some pages just had a few sentences and he used foul language liberally.

I want to write in first person because it feels less formal and more like me.

I want to write about what works for me as a coach.

I want to tell you what I most don't want you to know — that I doubt myself and my work. That it hurts when someone tells me my work sucks. That I worry that everything I have ever done is nonsense. That being a coach is a racket.

I want to write something that resonates with you and with me and therefore connects us in some agreement. I love it when we agree and then we can get to work. I can take a look into your mind and see what is going on. I want to write about your mind so you can say "yes" when I describe it and then agree that something can be done to make it less painful.

I want to write a book that my kids will read someday and learn at least one thing about their mom and one thing about themselves.

I want to write "self help" not "Brooke Help". After you read this book, I want you to help yourself and not think you need to hire me to be helped. I want you to find your own inspiration to find your own answers within you.

I want to write you a love letter from yourself so you will love yourself more and know how amazing you are. I want to write something that helps you create something that I want to buy and be a part of.

I want to write a book that feels good in my hands and in my heart.

I don't want you to have to indulge me, I want to indulge you.

Inspiration

Where does our inspiration come from? I used to wait for it. I used to wonder where it was and why it hadn't come for awhile. I would sit in my life, drinking wine and watching TV, waiting.

And then one day I realized that if I were inspiration, I wouldn't come to me either. I didn't appear to be ready to be inspired. Low on energy and vigor, inspiration had gone elsewhere to be realized. I was talking on the phone to my friend and told her that I was tired of waiting. I told her it was time to create some inspiration.

I needed to create some inspiration by getting back to work.

So I created a bunch of thoughts that motivated me to create. I thought them and lived them and then created some evidence for them. I created a class called "The 42-Day Jumpstart" that my clients loved. I created a three-series classed titled "The Art of Self Coaching," and then I started writing this book.

It really happened by changing one thought. The thought went from: *"I am waiting to be inspired"* to *"I am creating my own in-*

spiration." It feels way better and gives me such better results.

The added benefit is that it puts me in control and in power of my own life. I feel stronger and more capable. And, obviously, the results show it. When I get an email saying that my class helped, I know it isn't just a luxury to be in charge of my own inspiration, but it is my responsibility to give what I've got to the world.

It Was Always Meant to Happen that Way

For the past few years I have had a mantra: "That was meant to happen."

Then, one of my clients improved upon it for me: "It was always meant to happen that way."

Say it about anything.

Anything you argue with yourself about.

Say it about your horrible, cringe-worthy past.

Say it about yesterday.

Say it about your weight, your lack of money, your daughter who's failing math.

The minute you say it, the minute you believe it, peace happens.

Resistance leaves. A higher, more intelligent force enters the room.

And smiles.

Live You

It is not what you do, it's who you are when you are doing it.

Find something and throw yourself at it with all your might.

Dig.

Go in.

Find the best part of you and apply it to your task at hand.

What you are doing today may not end up being what you stay with long term but you will have learned how to live in your highest gear.

Then you can take that meta-skill into your next endeavor.

Even if you don't like your current job or body, give it your best.

Get really skilled at giving 100%.

Then, a day may come when you have the opportunity to work at your dream job, start your own business, lose 50 pounds, or meet the person you have been waiting for, for so long.

Be ready.

Be up to speed.

Show up on fire where you are.

Now.

Dancing with Impulse

Impulsive is a word I use to describe myself. Many of my impulses have been awesome, risk taking wonders that have led me to a business that makes me very good money and relationships that are meaningful and true.

But some of my impulses have not served me. Impulses to buy expensive things I don't really need or ultimately want. Impulses to drink too much wine or eat too much food or skip a dentist appt.

I have learned to dance with my impulses. Instead of pushing them away, I ask them to dance with me. I lead the dance. I include the impulse and feel it and move with it, and then guide it. I engage with it without succumbing to it. And then I tire of dance and thank the impulse and quietly walk away.

Risking Relationships as a Coach

As your coach, I am not your friend.

People do not pay me to be their friends; they pay me to tell them the truth.

We don't always tell our friends the real, whole truth we see about their lives. Often, we are afraid (rightly so) it might risk the relationship. And, quite frankly, how they live their lives is not really our business.

As a coach and as a trainer of coaches, I do get paid to tell the truth. I get paid to see it from a clean perspective, and then tell it how I see it.

This does risk the relationship.

I have had clients leave (and later come back) because I have told them the truth the way I see it.

Sometimes the truth is hard to hear, even when it is said with kindness and love.

Sometimes it is easier to be angry with me than to consider the perspective I have.

When a student sends me her work and tells me it is her best (and I know it isn't), I usually tell them I know it isn't.

When they tell me they can't get clients because of the economy, I tell them straight up they are lying to themselves, and then I ask them what they have done to build their business in the past week.

When they tell me that there is no way to lose weight permanently, and I know there is ample evidence to the contrary, I am not too shy to point that out.

Friends will come into your story with you and comfort you. And sometimes you need just that.

But, as your coach, I will not come into your story. I will stay on the outside and tell you what I see.

And, even if you don't like what you hear, I love you enough to say it.

I care enough about you to risk the relationship, to tell you the truth.

That is the kind of coaching that saved my life and that is the kind of coach I want to be.

The Choice

My son didn't do so well on that test he studied so hard for.

He gulped back tears as he told me.

I didn't react.

I asked why.

He said he didn't know.

And then in the car, later, I told him this:

> *Everything that you do in your life that seems like failure*
> *gives you a choice.*
> *You can either use it to love yourself more or less.*
> *There is no other option.*

So, my beloved son who hung the moon, what will your choice be today?

That's so hard, Mom.

I know, buddy.

But can you imagine if you started loving yourself each

time you make a mistake or miss a goal or do poorly on a test or say something you didn't mean? Can you imagine how you would feel about yourself and how much kinder a person you would be if you always chose love?

Yes, Mom. It feels waaaaay better.

In ten years you won't remember the grade you got on that test, but you will remember and you will feel the love you chose.

Maybe that's the real test.

Victims Are Not Vulnerable

People who play the victim role in their lives love to feel self-pity.

They want you to think that what "happened" to them is who they are. They want to show you how wounded they are so you can use your precious life energy tip toeing around their vulnerability.

Victims are passive aggressive. When you don't acknowledge their old pain, they get pissed.

Then you feel guilty.

The gift that keeps on giving.

How could you?

After all they have done for you?

After all they have been through?

They want you to see them as fragile.

By so doing, they don't have to put themselves back together.

Don't fall for it.

Victims are not vulnerable.

They just haven't done their work.

Do yours.

Too Much Thought Work

Sometimes I take clients from completely unconscious to obsessively analytical.

They come to me not even knowing that their thoughts cause their feelings, and then they somehow start sitting on the sidelines of their life watching and analyzing each and every thought they have.

They use coaching as further proof that they can get nowhere they want to be in their life.

I gently (okay, so not-so-gently), adjust them back by telling them this:

Become aware of your thoughts and how they affect your life.

Create some new thoughts to cultivate your new life.

> *GET OFF YOUR BUTT AND BUILD SOME*
> *EVIDENCE FOR YOUR NEW THOUGHT.*

If your new thought is: *"I can make this relationship work."*

Then do it.

Don't wait to see if love comes to you.

Love them, As in a verb, as in action. Love them to prove it will work. Love them to prove to yourself you do love them.

Don't watch your thought and then wait and see what happens. Create your thoughts and let those new thoughts fuel your ACTION.

Stop creating excuses to do more coaching, more healing, and more considering.

Do something.

First, clean up your thinking.

Second, work your butt off.

Repeat.

The Ego Doesn't Like Simplicity

"Simplicity is the ultimate in sophistication." ~Leonardo DaVinci

I have been doing a lot of self coaching on the idea of simplicity. I really want my life to be and stay simple. I want my money to be simplified in terms of the number of accounts I have. I want my stuff to be simplified so it isn't so hard for me to decide what to wear or what game to play or what wine glass to serve wine in. I want my recipes to be simplified so I can easily find a healthful meal to feed my family.

So why isn't it?

Why is much of my life so complicated? Why do I have so much stuff and so many broker statements and so many glasses?

There must be a reason.

I think on some level I feel, as an adult, my life should be complicated. That is such a ridiculous thought to say out loud, but I really think it's true. Mortgages and taxes and ROI, and scheduling our busy lives are all part of being an adult.

But what if it isn't?

What if that is just a belief that is no longer necessary?

What if life really is just like kindergarten?

I think it might be:

> Eat only when you are hungry.
>
> Be kind.
>
> Spend less than you earn.
>
> Help people.
>
> Love your family.
>
> Less is more.

As I move forward in my life, I see that the simpler my life is, the more I am able to appreciate it and be in it.

Fewer appointments, less busy-ness, less obligation.

The Ego in me doesn't like this. It doesn't feel good with a Tuesday afternoon with nothing important or sophisticated to do.

But my soul loves it. Looking out the window at the egoless Cherry Blossom Tree with nowhere to go and nothing to do, living a full and inspired life, on purpose.

The Moment after an Unanswered Craving

This chapter is a journal entry I shared with my "42-Day Jumpstart" students who requested it:

There is a moment after an unanswered craving. A single moment...

This moment of stopping and feeling requires consciousness and truth.

Sometimes it feels easier to pretend...

> Pretend I'm still hungry when I'm not.
>
> Pretend that food tasting good is more important than life tasting good.
>
> Telling myself that I don't matter.
>
> Telling myself I can get away with it.

When I am able to experience these moments more — I feel more . . .

> ~intimate with myself
>
> ~more awake, and
>
> ~more vulnerable.

The vulnerable part is scary sometimes. When I embrace it, I feel as if I am embracing myself and my precious vulnerability instead of turning my back on myself.

And it is always worth it.

Long term, it is always worth it.

That Was Meant To Happen

This is my mantra: That was meant to happen.

I think I picked it up when I started studying Byron Katie's work.

One day, I just noticed how often I say this in my head.

How brilliantly it sets me free, every time.

It releases me from my argument with the past. That argument I have never (not once) won.

When things go wrong or someone doesn't think I am fabulous, it was meant to happen.

When I am late for a meeting or the phone doesn't work for my telecourse, it was meant to happen.

When my son brings home an "F" or the kids tease him at school, it was meant to happen.

When I overeat pizza, it was meant to happen.

And when my best friend sends me a letter that says: "Because of you, I became a happier person."

And means it.

That was meant to happen.

It's So Worth It

Sometimes we avoid pain and we know it.

We know we are eating the food to avoid the sadness.

We know we are overspending to avoid the fear.

The pain seems so much more difficult than the cookies.

But it's not.

The pain covered in cookies becomes pain covered in fat covered in more pain.

Pain is hard.

To go through and feel the emotion instead of avoiding/distracting takes courage.

Sometimes we say, "Just this once I will avoid it. I'm too tired today."

We think that it doesn't matter.

It does.

We abandon ourselves.

We look away from our own suffering.

And when we do it on purpose, it hurts more, not less.

Be willing to feel what is true. Sometimes what is true is:

anger

sadness

shame

fear

loneliness

boredom

anxiety

When we say yes to the truth and feel what is real, we connect and learn to have intimacy with ourselves — our true selves.

That connection is not something you can buy.

It is something you earn.

Each time.

And it is so worth it.

Effort vs. Struggle

Not long ago I had a one-day seminar with my coach trainees. These are the women who have studied all my materials and tools on top of already being certified through another organization.

You know what we spent most of that day working on?

Goal-Setting.

It is so interesting how many of us full time coaches forget to do the basic techniques that are tried and true. It seems the more we get into thought work and being present, the less we want to focus on our futures and creating our lives.

I asked each of the coaches to set a financial goal for the coming year. I asked them to pick a dollar amount they wanted to generate (knowing this request would get resistance). Sure enough, I got push back from some of them. In general, they said, "What if you don't want anything more? What if I am perfectly happy with the amount of money I have right now? Why should I have to write a goal of getting more?"

Interesting.

Many of us are conditioned to want from a place of lack. We write goals and lists of things we want, feeling badly as we write them. Some of us believe that if we want more that we are somehow not appreciating what we have right now.

I couldn't disagree more.

I believe the only way to want (and write goals) is from a place of abundance. I encourage my clients to write lists of things they want. On this list, they should include the things they want and already have. For example: I want an awesome relationship with my husband. I already have this and I want it. I want it from a place of abundance and the wanting feels good.

Wanting is an amazing, inspiring, enlivening force when we want from a place of abundance. It can be exciting and energizing to think about what we want for our lives. It opens us up to our own growth and creativity to set big goals and cultivate the new thinking required to achieve them.

"But," you may be asking, "when is enough enough?"

Right now.

I have enough in this moment, and I love wanting more from a place of enough.

Wanting is only exhausting when we believe we can't have what we want or that if we don't have it, we can't be happy.

Wanting is what keeps life moving. Wanting what is and wanting what will be...

I have and want more joy.

I have and want more love.

I have and want more Chris, money, yoga, clients, and family time.

I have and want this life.

And from abundance I will have it.

And want even more....

You Do Not Have to Be Good

This is the first line in a Mary Oliver poem.

This one line is so empowering, freeing, and energizing.

When I heard "You do not have to be good," read aloud, I almost fell over.

I don't?

Really?

Are you sure?

Who says?

I noticed how this one thought made me feel and act.

If I don't have to be good, I am going to do it.

I am not going to begrudge myself when I am not good.

I am not going to quit, just because I am not any good at it.

What does it mean for us if we don't have to be good? We have all been told and conditioned to believe we need to behave like good girls, do good homework, be good at work, be good at relationships, and be good citizens.

Many of us can't embrace the part of us that isn't good, the part of us that can't spell or eat -2 to 2 or have grace socially. (Or the part that writes a fragment instead of a sentence) But maybe that's the point. Maybe the point isn't just to embrace the part of us that is amazing, but also the part of us that just isn't any good.

I could like, or maybe even love, myself when I am not a good girl?

I don't have to be good?

Thanks for letting me know.

That changes everything.

What Is Here to Teach You?

"Nothing ever goes away until it has taught us what we need to know.
Even if we run a hundred miles an hour to the other side of the continent,
we find the very same problem awaiting us when we arrive."
~Pema Chodron

Emotional overeating (what I call fog eating) is one of the best teachers I have ever had. The process (eating lots of food when I wasn't hungry) and the results (being overweight) led me into myself. I don't know if I would have ever found the life I am currently living and the person I currently am without this education.

Make no mistake; I didn't see it this way when I was knee-deep into it. I used to curse the fact that I was overweight and obsessed with food. I used to think it meant something was wrong with me. Why could my best friend, Erika, eat half her frozen yogurt and then throw it away? Why did I have to inhale it and wish I had more? I felt weak and inadequate.

Overeating was painful. It wouldn't go away. I would starve myself and lose weight for a short period of time, but my relentless teacher would come back and ask me to do the work again and again. It was much like a professor who requires a paper be rewritten until they are sure you have learned the material. I tried all the tricks to get it done. I went on new diets. I tried to embrace being overweight. I tried working out three times a day. But these attempts were never acceptable to my teacher. I had not learned what I needed to learn and so the problem remained.

It wasn't until I did the freeing work of asking myself, "Why?" that I begun to learn what I needed to know. Once I moved past the behavior and results (which were just symptoms of my thinking) and focused on the cause, I began to learn about the person I really am. I learned to listen and trust my body. I learned to pay attention to myself and find out what really mattered to my soul. I uncovered and removed programming I had received as a child that was not helpful or even true for me anymore. I found out what I needed to know.

And the teacher went away.

I no longer have an issue with overeating and hating my body. I no longer obsess about food or the size of my jeans. I now know why I did. I know now, on a much deeper level, who I am and what I want.

I am so thankful for the relentless teacher of overeating.

For you, it may be something different that keeps coming up again and again in your life. Maybe, like me, you tell yourself that you are weak because you can't overcome this issue. But what if you are wrong? What if this "issue" with money or men or yelling or drinking is only a guide, a teacher trying to get your attention? What if it is here on purpose to teach you what you need to know to live an even bigger life?

Maybe someday you will thank the current problem you curse.

Maybe it will end up being the best teacher you've ever had.

The Best Things in Life Are Created, Not Bought

I am currently reading Katrina Kenison's book, *The Gift of an Ordinary Day*. I am really enjoying her insights about parenting and spending time with her family. She reminds me to slow down and pay attention to the moments that will all too soon be memories:

My son opening the curtains in our hotel room and whispering, "Thank you, world," when he saw the view we had of Disneyland was precious. But, just as precious, was the drive to soccer practice where he confided to me that he had fun playing at recess.

The other day, while the four of us watched Survivor as a family, I found myself staring at my younger son's face. I can't believe how beautiful he is. I can't believe he came from my body. I am overwhelmed, in this ordinary moment, with the magnificence of my baby boy's face.

And there is so much more.....

My son reaching to hold my hand as we walk into the grocery store.

My husband's beautiful blue eyes when he opens them first thing in the morning.

The fist-bump between the soccer coach and Christian after a good practice.

The parent–teacher conference where she tells us how much she enjoys Connor.

My brother's face after driving two hours to watch Christian play.

The sound of wrestling between dad and son from an upstairs room.

My mother, throwing her head back to laugh after a funny comment I make.

Christian holding the door open for me.

As I write this, it is the holiday season and I am overwhelmed with gratitude for all the gifts in my life. I have so many opportunities to create a wealth of memories and connections without ever stepping into a store or placing an order on line.

You are creating your own life right now with the thoughts you think and things you do. You may be creating so much more than you realize, just by being who you are. So take a moment over the next few months and create moments of love and joy by noticing what is already there. An ordinary day, paid attention to, just might be magnificent.

Stop Trying to Be Who You Are Not

I was reading *O* magazine while at my son's soccer practice yesterday. I had to stop and go find a pen so I could underline half of the article. I want to just copy it here and stay out of it, but there is that whole copyright issue so here is the gist of what I took away from Anne Lamott's article, "Where Do I Start?"

Many of my Self-Coaching clients come to me and want to "find themselves" as if they are somewhere else than where they are in this moment. I try to help them see that they are here. They are found. This is it, folks, front and center. Some of us pretend to be lost, because we aren't living in truth. Anne suggests that the way we discover ourselves, and find the happiness that already resides within, is to "gently stop being who we aren't."

Genius.

Notice her use of the word, "gently."

We are not beating ourselves into submission, we are gently letting go of anything non-authentic. We do it through peace, not war. Kindness is the path inward to ourselves.

Next, she reminds us that, "You have to make mistakes to find out who you aren't."

It is like what I tell my clients: If you live and tell your truth, the people who are meant to be in your life will be there. If you try something and it doesn't resonate with you, change course and do something drastically different with no regard to "what other people might think."

I have made more mistakes than most of the people I know. Big, expensive, painful mistakes. But now I know. I know that was the wrong direction and I have corrected. I have come back to myself.

I have stopped being who I am not.

But I had to try out who I am not, to discover just exactly who I am.

No regrets.

Just kindness, gently becoming more me with each and every disastrous mistake.

You Can't Get Enough... of Something You Don't Really Want

I first heard this from one of my favorite authors, Geneen Roth. She was talking about binge eating and describing why we keep eating huge amounts of food beyond fullness and sometimes even beyond feeling sick. She explained: We are trying to get something we desperately want, from something that can't give it to us.

In all my years of working on myself and with my clients in my practice, I have found this to be a common, unevaluated pattern. We are never going to get love from an Oreo, commitment from an uninterested man, or true fulfillment from being a workaholic. Many of us desperately try harder and harder—but it is never enough.

Think about any overindulgence in your life.

What are you *really* wanting?

Things Most People Don't Say on Their Deathbed

I wish I would have been twenty pounds thinner.

I wish I would have looked better in a bikini.

I wish I would have gotten some Botox for these wrinkles.

I wish I drove a better car.

If only my house had been bigger.

I should have worn better jeans and carried a better purse.

I wish my hair would have been thicker.

I wish I would have spent less time with my kids.

I should have complained to my husband more.

I should have spent less time cuddling with my dog.

I should have made my boss happier.

I should have worked more weekends.

I should have cleaned out the garage.

I should have bought more stuff.

I imagine most people say things like:

*I wish I would have taken better care of myself,
my health and my body.*

I don't want to leave.

I love you.

I want more time.

Just sit with me.

I want to BE here with you.

I love you.
I love you.
I love you.

Why wait?

What are *you* saying today?

Hard Work

I have two sons, Christian and Connor.

Connor is my youngest at eight years-old. He is so naturally talented at most things that my husband and I spend a lot of time looking at each other wondering where he came from. He was reading the TV at two years old, memorizing time tables at six, and winning soccer games almost single-handedly by seven. He doesn't really have to study or practice, he just shows up and shines.

Christian, on the other hand, works his butt off to get the same results. He has to study and read and re-study and practice to get the results he wants. He puts hours into practicing soccer to get the same results as his brother gets with very little practice. He has to read for two hours to get through the same amount of pages his brother reads in thirty minutes. He puts out so much effort for the exact same reward.

It is frustrating for him.

All I can do is agree with him. It might be difficult having Connor as a brother when you are only one year apart and very competitive.

But here is what I have noticed....

Christian knows how to work. That boy can work hard. He has a work ethic that will carry him very far in this life. He is determined to be the best he can be and he is willing to put in the time and effort to make sure that happens.

I try to explain to him what a gift this is. I try to teach him that working hard and accomplishing things on your own sweat is what creates the best feeling in the world: pride. He gets to own his accomplishments from a deeper place because he worked so hard for them. He is developing his "overcome" muscles. He is learning to manage his emotions and not let them manage him. He is building the tools to put in a tool belt that will serve him as a man.

Connor has a much harder time when faced with an obstacle. He is so used to being the best with so little effort that when he isn't "winning" he has a complete fit. He doesn't see that as a cue to work harder, he sees it as a cue that something has gone wrong. He is much more apt to quit. He is much more prone to acting out his emotions in self-destructive ways.

I try to teach Connor the tools I know so he can overcome his life's obstacles. I coach him. I explain to him that if he can take his natural talent and combine it with a work ethic, there will be very little he can't do in this life. It is much harder for him to understand. His experience and belief system supports things coming easy.

As I watch my boys, who are so very different, I am fascinated. I know adults who have similar struggles. I have clients who share similar beliefs. As I think about this, I am determined to find a way to teach both of my kids the value of hard work. Working hard for yourself and something you believe in is powerful stuff. It feels amazing. It develops your character.

I am not talking about struggle. I am not talking about the kind of work that spins you in circles and feels defeating. I am talking about not feeling sorry for yourself when it doesn't come easily. I am talking about being grateful when you accomplish something that took a bit more effort than the next person to accomplish.

The truth is…you don't know what went into anyone's accomplishment.

The other day, someone told Christian he was the best nine-year-old goalie they had ever seen. They said, "It must be wonderful to have so much talent at such a young age."

Little did they know, Christian made his talent. He created it with hours of practice and very hard work.

When is the last time you looked at someone with "talent" or "success" and thought how nice it must be for them to have so much?

Did you chalk it up to luck or genetics or brains?

Might have just been some old-fashioned hard work.

Hard work feels good.

If you aren't already, you should try it.

What Are You Becoming?

This question rocks: What are you becoming?

Answer it.

As a coach, I love questions. I know that the better the questions we ask ourselves the better thoughts we think. About six months ago I started asking myself, "What is perfect about this?" This question, asked repeatedly, has changed my whole life. It helps me look at problems with potential and therefore find amazing and unexpected solutions. I have taught this question and asked this question to each person I work with in my practice.

And now, I have a new favorite question.

Who am I becoming?

I love the possibility of it. I love the promise of it. I love the future-focus of it.

It infers growth and movement and realized potential.

Write this question at the top of a blank page and then answer it.

I did. Here is s sampling:

I am becoming more of who I am and who I am meant to be.

I am becoming a better and more outrageous mother.

A fairly good water skier.

An incredible abundance attractor.

A more available and considerate friend.

Much more social.

A yogi.

Unapologetic for who I really am.

An amazing and understanding wife.

More free and accepting.

A "guided" coach capable of genuinely helping others in even just one hour.

An amazing athlete.

A more loving, honest daughter.

A contributor.

What are you becoming?

What Are You Asking Yourself?

I just went on a week-long houseboat vacation. I lived in my bathing suit. When I wasn't water skiing or swimming, I was sitting on the sundeck reading.

When I got home and looked at the pictures, I was astounded that I had been parading around in a bikini for a week with not one negative judgment towards myself. I had not beaten myself up once for my body.

Those of you who have suffered with your weight and body image know how miraculous this is.

I realized that my new programming has become natural at this point, and on this vacation I had only asked myself great questions.

Questions like:

Could it be any more beautiful here? How incredible are these kids? How fun is this? Who gets to have this much fun? Does water get any better for skiing? How could we get so lucky? Could my husband be any cuter, funnier, worse at Mexican Train?

I never asked myself why I wasn't skinnier or prettier. Not once.

Great questions. Great answers.

Awesome vacation.

Do it.

This Is Here to Help Me.

This is my new favorite thought: *This is here to help me.*

I like saying this about anything.

Try it. It feels good.

You lose money in the stock market.

"This is here to help me."

You gain five pounds.

"This is here to help me."

Someone is mean to you.

You lose a friend.

You get fired.

Your computer crashed.

You are confused by what to do with your life.

It is all here to help you.

Truly.

All part of the plan.

Perfect.

Helpful.

Important.

Intended.

It is 107 degrees here where I live and I have a mosquito
bite that won't stop itching.

This is here to help me.

It is what I need in this moment to live my life.

And I will.

My Lifetime of Deliberate Practice

I often get emails asking me how I know what I know and do what I do. I usually reply the same answer to everyone so I thought I would share it with anyone else who wonders about me as a coach.

I have spent my life reading self-help books. My first memory of getting hooked was when I was fifteen years old and breaking up with my boyfriend. I was in excruciating emotional pain because of unprocessed pain from my childhood. I went to the bookstore and bought Robin Norwood's book, *Women Who Love Too Much*. I started reading it in the tub that evening and didn't stop until the book was done and the water was cold. That book gave me tremendous relief. I immediately felt a deep love for Robin who clearly understood my pain. I was not alone.

Since that day, I have made it a life-long habit to go to the bookstore when I feel any type of emotional pain. This habit of "reading for relief" eventually turned into the habit of "reading for any dang reason at all." I mostly read non-fiction, self-help, and psychology. I have also been known to read a business book on the side. Authors have become my mentors, friends, confidants and saviors.

Now, you must know, when I read a book I really read it. I read it, underline it, think about it, question it, apply it, and live it for a while. I suspend my judgment on most ideas until I have tried them out for myself. I do the worksheets, practice the practices, and consider the concepts on a deep level. Many times I end up integrating the practices into my life and other times I toss out ideas that don't resonate with the way I live my life.

It always amuses me when someone, who has read my book, writes me and tells me it isn't working; as if my book could do the work for them. When I reply and ask if they are keeping the journals or writing down the thoughts, I am never surprised when they send back their list of excuses.

Knowledge not applied can't change your life.

But, take it from me, if you apply the knowledge that resonates with you from each book you read, you will have the life of your dreams before you know it. Let others who have gone before you show you the way.

That's how I do it and have done it, since I was fifteen years old.

Thank you, Robin.

How Does It Feel To Want?

My friend, Meadow, pointed out to me that when I want something, I feel good. She noted that most people feel crappy when they want.

The difference?

Many people don't believe they can have what they want.

I do.

When I want something, I believe I will someday have it. Now or later doesn't matter. I get excited at the prospect of it so I don't need it right this second to feel great about it.

I want the new iPhone. I want a pair of black Jimmy Choo heels I saw at Foot Candy. I want to go water skiing on Thursday with my friend Dava. I want to buy a boat. I want to go on another date with my husband.

I want more peace in the world.

I want the economy to flourish.

I want everyone to feel as proud to be an American as I do.

I want to help more people become free of extra weight and self punishment.

I want us all to make even more money and give even more away.

Wanting excites me.

If, when you think about what you want, you feel any negative emotion; my guess is you will never get it. That is not how the universe works. You get to want from a place of positive attraction, and then there is nothing that you can't have.

But *when* you "get" it doesn't matter, because you already feel that it's yours.

Oh No . . . Not Again!

"I can't believe I gained this weight back again."

"I can't believe I ran this credit card up again."

"I can't believe I dated another jerk."

"I know better. I can't get anything right. I am a failure. I will NEVER get it. Something is wrong with me."

Blah Blah Blah . . .

Enough with the drama already.

Aren't you tired of treating yourself like you suck?

I remember doing this to myself over and over and over. I see my clients do it to themselves.

Listen, you must stop beating yourself up.

The problem is not that you over-ate or that you gained seventy pounds back. The problem is not that you over-spend or are in credit card debt.

The problem is that you use this as evidence that you aren't worthy or good enough to live the life of your dreams.

Gaining all the weight back that you lost means only one thing…(and there is no drum roll-there is no drama).

It means you are still trying to get your attention to some of your own self work.

You aren't done with you yet. You have more to learn about you. You have more connection to create with your own self.

Running up your credit cards again, when you promised yourself you wouldn't, is just INTERESTING. It is an opportunity to get to know WHY. Learn about yourself and why you go unconscious in your own life.

Practice the tools that help you manage your mind and your thoughts. Keep practicing. You might gain the weight back ten times before you really get the hang of it…

Who Cares?

Be nice to yourself and give yourself time to go deeper. Notice those ridiculous and mean thoughts you think.

For a while, your pattern may look like this:

Get the hang of it. See the cool result in your life. Screw it all up completely by checking out. Get the hang of it. (repeat)

You might have to do this twenty times before, one day, you realize that you haven't screwed it up in years.

But, by that time, you will be screwing up something completely new and . . .

One more opportunity to go deeper into your self.

Your life.

Be willing to do it again and again and again.

Do it with understanding and kindness.

Again.

What Is Supposed to Happen . . .Does.

Today, while cleaning my patio with my jet spray hose, I hosed a hummingbird nest from within one of our table umbrellas.

I didn't realize what I had done until the mama came and frantically buzzed around my head. It was horrible. She kept looking for the nest. I am not sure how many eggs were in there, but I am pretty sure none of them will make it.

An hour later I saw her flying around looking for it again.

This was devastating to me.

My husband told me that it was an accident and that she would lay more eggs.

As I continued to obsess about it, he told me that it was in the past and there was nothing I could do about it now. He hugged me and held me. He helped me put the nest back in case she wanted to reuse it. He talked about it with me endlessly.

I still felt awful.

Hummingbirds are so beautiful and dainty and small. I felt like a big predator.

I went to yoga and on the way down I coached myself. I monitored my thoughts and saw how painful they were. I reminded myself that worrying about it would not help. I tried to give myself a break and worked through my self-coaching model.

When I got to yoga, I felt slightly better.

Then, as we began to breathe deeply, this thought came to me: *"What is supposed to happen...does."*

That nest was supposed to get sprayed out of the umbrella.

I was the one who was supposed to do it.

How do I know this?

Because that is exactly what happened.

So, instead of asking myself why this was supposed to happen, I dedicated the rest of my yoga practice to just being in the moment of it having happened. I breathed it in and accepted it. I stopped arguing with the past I could not change.

That nest was supposed to be unknowingly destroyed.

There is no use in blaming or hating or fighting or eating over it.

Mama bird was supposed to have that experience.

I was supposed to have this one.

That is what is.

Not all endings are happy. Not all things turn out so we can feel good.

Sometimes we can't find a "bright side" or the "good news," and maybe we aren't supposed to.

Maybe we can just find peace in the way things are.

I love that mama hummingbird, and I didn't even know I loved her.

I didn't know I would feel so much love today…

What is supposed to happen…does.

Relax

You can either make your habits or your habits can make you. We all seem to know this and yet sometimes we feel as if we can't control our habits. There are things we seem to do regularly that we don't know how to stop.

When it comes to my weight-loss clients, I often tell them if they want to know why they overeat — stop overeating. As soon as you stop doing the bad habit or taking the negative action, it will be very clear why you do it in the first place. The first thing you will notice is the feeling that comes up.

When my clients stop overeating they are typically bombarded with negative emotion. Their knee jerk reaction after years of practice is to fight the emotion, escape the emotion, or bury the emotion. Picking up more food is a way to escape the emotion temporarily. BUT if we are willing — and many of us are — to RELAX INTO THE EMOTION and feel it deeply, we can watch it pass through us.

Eventually, as we get better at experiencing the truth of our emotional state, we can find the thought that is causing the feeling and then change it.

There is no negative emotion that can stand up to an embrace. Negative emotion is fed by the fight or the habit that compounds it. If I am feeling lonely and I overeat, I will feel even more so when the eating is done. Most likely I will get an added dose of shame and frustration after the food coma passes.

No matter what the unwanted action is you have in your life, you can start to eliminate it by doing this process:

1. Stop taking the action.

2. Notice the desire to "fight" or use "willpower" against the emotion that arises (you will typically lose this battle).

3. Relax into the underlying emotion and breathe. Notice the emotion from the witness perspective.

4. Keep relaxing and keep breathing and notice the thoughts that come up.

5. Write down the thought.

6. Acknowledge that if you want to change the habit, you must change the thought.

Permanent change is never made by fighting or intense willpower. Long term loving change occurs when we relax and identify the cause.

Growth Is Not Comfortable

Anyone who has grown spiritually, mentally or physically knows that growth is not found in comfort.

My yoga teacher, Diana, said this when we were in pyramid pose the other day, and it exploded as a concept in my mind. I had heard this before, but it hit me deeply during this class in a whole new way. I laughed to myself when I thought about discomfort in my own life.

About ten years ago, when I was starting my first company in Colorado, I was very uncomfortable. I was having issues with my business partner and some of my employees. I called my very good friend to whine and cry about how uncomfortable I was. I will never forget what she said to me. "This is why I don't do all this crazy stuff you do — like opening businesses, Brooke. You always end up in these situations where you are struggling. I choose not to put myself through that."

When she said this to me, I literally felt jealous of her. I thought of her at home not having to deal with the mess of issues I was currently facing. I questioned my own judgment and my own complicated life.

Unfortunately, at this time, I did not have the coaching tools I have today. I was suffering and in tremendous discomfort. But now, as I look back on that painful time and many painful times since then, I can only high five myself for putting myself in those uncomfortable situations. I am so proud that I put myself out there in the ways that I did and failed miserably, sucked terribly, and made countless mistakes with people and with business. I am no longer jealous of my friend who sits at home in comfort. I see how far I have come, not in spite of the discomfort, but because of it.

As I get older, I notice that those opportunities for discomfort just don't come along as often. I don't have to try new things or start new schools or be the new employee anymore. I am established in my career and good at what I do and very comfortable in my family and community life. I can see how it might be tempting for me to stay in the comfort zone and not "do all the crazy" stuff anymore. But I know, especially now looking back, how I am a much better, deeper, complete Brooke Castillo because I did. I want to look back ten years from now and feel the same way.

I want to grow as much in the next decade as I did in the last. In order to do that, I will seek out things that I want and that also make me uncomfortable. For example, I am always uncomfortable for at least three poses on my yoga mat; I am uncomfortable learning how to ski the water ski buoys faster; I am uncomfortable making new friends when I have so many "comfortable" friends already. But I will continue. I will grow. I am not done growing. Are you?

I Cheated on Myself and Got Away with It

"I ate and didn't gain weight."
"I didn't floss and my teeth are fine."
"I cheated on my taxes and no one caught me."
"I lied and she didn't know."

These are actual quotes from clients of mine.

Can you see how they are completely missing the point?

When you cheat on yourself . . . you cheat on yourself.

You know.

You are the one.

The cheater and the cheated.

A double bummer if you ask me.

You deserve better and *you know it.*

Stumble Often

By your stumbling, the world is perfected.
~Sri Aruobindo

So what that you totally screwed it up. So you said the wrong thing. You wore the wrong outfit. You made out with the wrong guy. You ate the wrong food at the wrong time.

I make so many damn mistakes, I would have to hire a full time assistant to keep track.

But why would I? My mistakes are the only things that allow for my wins. I can't win sitting in the corner not wanting to do the wrong thing, follow the wrong path, make a mistake, make a complete ass of myself. I can't do that because this is the journey I am meant to be taking. This is the path I must stumble on in order to arrive at my destiny.

What the hell are you waiting for? So what that you have tried and it didn't work out? So what if what you said was something completely inappropriate? Say something different.

Stumble. Keep stumbling until you stumble yourself right into greatness.

Stumble hard and often

Then do it again.

Practice

What do you practice? What do you do over and over each day?

Whatever you're practicing — you are getting better at.

If you are practicing soccer (like my son), you are getting better at soccer.

If you are practicing video games (like my other son), you are becoming a better gamer.

Likewise, if you are practicing negative thoughts, you are getting better at thinking them.

If you are practicing being mean and cruel to yourself, you are getting good at self-abuse.

If you are practicing escaping your thoughts/feelings with alcohol or food, that is a skill you are perfecting.

Stop right now and watch your thoughts for a minute. Does this come naturally to you? Have you been practicing observing yourself from a place of compassion? Do you know where your mind tends to go when it is not being managed?

I have noticed a huge change in my mind's tendencies since I have begun practicing good-feeling thoughts. I used to take time to watch and write down all the thoughts that went through my mind when I was feeling incredibly depressed or anxious. I noticed that each and every thought was negative, mean and mostly untrue. After a few years of consciously managing my thoughts, I notice that now most of them are now supportive, positive, and true.

I have practiced thinking.

I have deliberately thought new, fresh, and good thoughts as a practice.

I have intentionally questioned and replaced negative feeling thoughts the minute they surface to my awareness.

As a result of this practice, I have gotten very good at this sport of mind management. I feel good most of the time.

At what do you want to get better?

Are you practicing?

"We learn by practice. Whether it means to learn to dance by practicing dancing or to learn to live by practicing living, the principles are the same. One becomes in some area an athlete of God."
~Martha Graham

Refuse the Thought

"Would you like another credit card?"

"No, thank you."

"Would you like a second helping of dessert?"

"No, thank you."

"Would you like a cigarette?"

"No, thank you."

We refuse things we don't want all the time. It is not hard to do. We just say no.

This is what I recommend we do with the negative thoughts that appear in our minds.

Just refuse the thought.

"No, thank you, not today. That thought doesn't feel good."

No matter how many times someone asks me if I want a cigarette, I am always going to politely decline. This may not deter them from asking over and over — just like a thought might reappear over and over. It doesn't matter though. As long as I don't accept it, I don't have to feel the effects of that negative habit or thought.

"You should work harder."

"No, thanks."

"You aren't good enough."

"No, thanks."

"You know you aren't going to be able to pull this off."

"No, thanks."

"You aren't really good at this."

"No, thanks."

"You should join the PTA."

"Seriously, no."

"You are the luckiest girl in the world."

"Don't mind if I do."

I Would Like to Excuse Myself from Your Business

I love the way this sounds.

I love that I can say this anytime I start getting into someone else's business.

Whether I am in their business because I think I know how they should live their life in some way, or I am in their business because I am believing they know how to live mine; I love that (if it feels bad) I can excuse myself.

The word excuse is the key here.

I am not yelling at them to stay the hell out of my business. I am not flipping them off because they won't do what I say.

I am saying "excuse me" as if slightly apologizing for my audacity to think I know more about how they should think or behave than they do. I am excusing myself as if from a meal or a party that I no longer want to partake in.

It's not violent nor angry. It is mannered and gentle. It is acknowledging that I have found myself in a place I do not want to be and will now excuse myself.

For example:

Someone feels offended and is expressing their outrage that I won't take them on as a client. They are ranting on and on about how it is my responsibility to help them and that I can't be so busy as to not take them on....

It is at this point that I excuse myself from their business.

Or another example:

I think my husband should medicate my mother-in-law when she is highly anxious. I am indignant about it and forcing him to listen to the list of perfect reasons I have to prove this is the best course of action. As we raise our voices in disagreement, I pause and say apologetically say to him,

"It is at this point that I would like to excuse myself from your business."

I have enough of my own business. I am in people's business for a living, helping them sort out their most intimate thoughts and their relationship with their own minds. I am invited into my kid's business, my friend's business, and I welcome the people I love into mine when appropriate.

For the other precious moments of my life — I want to excuse myself from other peoples' business.

The Measure of a Woman . . .

I was watching a TV program the other night and a young athlete was thanking his coach who had taught him so much by telling him, "The true measure of a man is in how much it takes to discourage him."

I love this quote. I love it even more when you replace man with woman:

"The true measure of a woman is in how much it takes to discourage her."

I have seen so many of my weight-loss clients work through issue after issue without allowing any setback discourage them. They go through injuries, overeating, negative thinking, criticism, weight gain, and loss without ever allowing discouragement to take over and lead them.

I am always in awe of this. I am always inspired when a client tells me that they "did their work" and didn't let the circumstances of their life dictate their result. Ultimately, these women lose weight and a lot of it. But much more importantly, they learn that they are the one in control of their interior experience and how they feel. They learn that discouragement is a feeling caused by a thought — not an inevitable result of working towards something they want.

I have also had many other clients let discouragement get to them from the first thing that "doesn't go their way." They might gain a pound, or miss a workout, or hear something negative from a friend and dive into a place of discouraged feelings, actions, and ultimately results. These clients tend to blame others for their feelings and results and feel sorry for themselves.

I love each of these clients equally, but I do notice that the ones who disallow discouragement ALWAYS are the ones who end up measuring their success on the scale and in their relationship with themselves.

How much does it take to discourage you?

Is the Bad Stuff Easier To Believe?

There is a quote in the movie *Pretty Woman* where Julia Robert's character says, "The bad stuff is so much easier to believe."

I think about this quote sometimes when I get ten positive emails and then one negative email. For some reason, that negative email is the one that sticks in my mind. Why the heck is that?

Sometimes when people say, "I am your biggest fan, I love your work." I find myself thinking that they don't really know me. But when I get a review saying " I didn't really like your book." I find myself thinking they are on to me, that they have figured out I am not a very good writer. As if by reflex, I give more credit to the negative review.

But after I sit with it and think about it, I find the facts and the real truth. The facts are: I have only received a handful of negative emails and reviews and hundreds of positive ones. Most of the negative reviews are more about the person writing them than about me. And most of the negative reviews are inaccurate when they describe why they didn't like my book. (For example, one woman said there were no new concepts in the book and another said they had wanted more discussion of diabetes.)

I think the reflex reaction is actually habitual. For many years I had the belief that I wasn't good enough. I spent years creating and looking for evidence to prove this belief. It was my way of being in the world to look for "bad reviews" to prove that I wasn't good enough, nor would I ever be good enough. So now, when this evidence falls in my lap, it is almost like I can't help it. It feels familiar to use it against myself.

Evidence against the belief still takes a bit of effort to believe. It is still not completely natural for me to immediately hear, accept and believe genuine compliments or praise. I have to remind myself to take it in, to pause long enough to listen, and not to dismiss such important feedback.

So, yes, I do agree with Julia's in *Pretty Woman* when she says the bad stuff is easier to believe. It is the easy, unconscious, and painful way to live. So many of us have lived this way for so long that we have to make an effort not to. I do this for a living. I do work every single day on my thoughts. And still I have to stop and remind myself of the facts and the truth of what each review, person, or email is saying.

I think it is important to hear all the feedback and listen to what each person is saying. Some of the negative stuff is true and can be used in a constructive way to improve ourselves. This is very different than blindly believing the negative just because it is easier.

My new policy is to take each and every positive email I get, read it thoroughly and let it sink in. If someone has taken the time to write me and generously share their positive thoughts, then I can take the time and effort it requires to believe what they are telling me.

The bad stuff is easier to believe, but the good stuff is so much better!

Make the effort.

Kids

I love hanging with my kids. They don't talk about the economy or the housing prices (enough already). They don't worry about the stock market or the unemployment rates. They could care less how much Jessica Simpson weighs and they certainly don't want to talk about who, in government, isn't paying their taxes.

They want to know about the best movie in the theater right now. They want to know if a squirrel or a dog would win in a mile-long race. They want to know when they can go swimming and why ants work so hard. They want to hang out with me and their dad and play Monopoly and Uno. They think a sponge can live in a pineapple under the sea.

Yesterday I watched Christian play in three different soccer games. He was so in the moment with his friends and that ball. He didn't even notice me cheering hysterically on the sidelines. He wasn't worried. He isn't worried.

"Worry pretends to be necessary," said Eckhart Tolle in his book *A New Earth*.

I think he was right.

We learn to worry. We think we should worry because everyone else is. We think that if we worry we can prevent "bad" things from happening to us.

Of course, the opposite is true. When we worry, we attract the things we are concentrating on pushing against.

Being in the moment and keeping thoughts positive and cleaned-up doesn't mean we abdicate responsibility and sign an interest-only mortgage we can't afford.

It means we don't.

Think about it.

What we have is what we need.

Buying something we can't afford is an action taken from negative thinking.

Worrying endlessly if you lose your job is a feeling triggered by negative thinking and has no upside and a lot of downside.

Watch your kids and learn how to be in the moment.

Learn how not to worry.

They can show you how.

9 Don't Have to Be Better Than 9 Am

The other day I was doing some deep work on myself. I was having a hard time with a personal issue and I kept thinking: *I wish I was more patient and kind.* This thought was very painful because it was essentially telling me, I'm not good enough the way I am.

The truth is I am not more patient and more kind than I am. I am not more patient and kind than my thoughts drive me to be. I found this out when I brainstormed better-feeling thoughts. When I came across: "You don't have to be better than you are," a huge sense of relief washed over me.

Pretending never works out well for me. I am a straight shooter, and I say it like it is. You never have to wonder if I am upset because I will come right out and tell you how I feel. So, when I try to pretend I am more kind or more patient than I am, I have a negative physical reaction in my body. It isn't the truth.

The truth always feels better than pretending.

So does this mean I can be rude and insensitive and impatient with people and just write it off as being my "truth"?

Well, I guess I could, but that is equally painful. I do not like it when other people feel hurt or upset, and I don't want to trigger them to feel this way. What it does mean is that I can accept what I am feeling in this moment whether it be impatience or unkindness. I can accept it instead of fighting against it. This DOES NOT mean I have to act on it. It means I can find the thoughts that cause these feelings and get to the root of it.

This is much more kind to myself. It is much more patient to take the time to feel what is going on with me and accept that this is what is true for me in this moment. I don't have to fight it. I can work with it and consciously make choices that serve me.

As soon as I did this work and found this thought, I felt loving and patient and kind with myself. Of course, from this space, I was much more patient and kind with the people close to me.

I don't have to be better than I am.

Thank goodness.

My Own Thought Work

I really do practice what I preach most of the time. I do a lot of thought work on myself, and when I don't, I can really feel the difference. I start thinking so many thoughts that aren't true and then I end up feeling a bunch of negative feelings. I thought I would share a bit of my own thought work with you in hopes that it will help you when you are doing some of your own work.

My mother-in-law, Nancy, has moved in with us. Nancy has terminal cancer. They told us three years ago that she had two weeks to live and she is still with us and going quite strong! She is such a rock star.

Anyway, Nancy moved in with us about six weeks ago and I have had many thoughts about it since. I have thought the following very unhelpful thoughts:

I hate seeing her like this. She shouldn't be dying. She shouldn't be in so much pain. She shouldn't be so mean to me. She shouldn't have to go through this.

When I think this way, I get angry and sad. Most of the time she doesn't recognize us and realize where she is. She has a hard time understanding the basic information we tell her. She is not the Nancy that we have all known before she got sick. As a mother-in-law, she was great. She was always very supportive of me and my marriage to her son. She always welcomed me with open arms and was kind and loving to me and my family.

Now that she is sick, she does many out-of-character things. One minute she will be yelling at me for not bathing her properly, and the next minute she is trying to get me to sneak her in some cigarettes. She will ask me who the guy is that comes into her room (Chris, her son) and then she will tell me about her second husband (she was only married once).

Since she moved in, I have felt so many emotions because I have thought so many thoughts. When I was doing my thought work I came up with a thought that has turned it all around for me. The thought is:

I am growing as a person by being on this journey with Nancy.

It feels so true and good and freeing. This thought allows me to be with what *is* instead of arguing with it or wishing it different. I get relief just reading it now.

The other thought that saves me from feeling badly is:

This is so funny.

When she gets mad at me and yells at me or when she wakes up at midnight wanting ice cream, Chris and I have learned to find the humor in it. We find that laughing is so much better than crying in every single way. When she comes upstairs and calls me Billy and treats Chris like the maintenance man, we just smile and giggle with each other. We don't take it personally. We get as much enjoyment with her as we can.

Everything is exactly as it should be. I am growing and learning and laughing along the way. I can see how this circumstance, based on my thoughts, could wear me out and depress me. I have worked with many clients who have gained significant amounts of weight caring for a dying parent, and it is understandable how this might happen if thoughts go unchecked.

I can't change my circumstance: Nancy weighs about 90 pounds and she use to weigh 160. She sleeps about 20 hours a day. She is grumpy sometimes. But I can change my thoughts. And I will.

She still knows how to laugh.

And I will laugh with her for as long as she can.

Michelangelo

For those of you who don't know, I am homeschooling my son, Connor, this year. It is actually very good for me to retake third grade. I missed most of it the first time.

Today I learned something that blew my mind: Michelangelo hated painting the ceiling of the Sistine Chapel. Hated it.

If I had been his coach, I would have asked him why.

He would have told me that his boss was a tyrant and that he didn't see himself as a painter. He believed he was a sculptor. He would have told me he missed his family in Florence and that the pay was inconsistent.

Then, as his coach, I might have asked him why he didn't quit.

I know — I am so glad I wasn't his coach.

The ceiling of the Sistine Chapel is one of the most inspired and beautiful things I have ever seen. How could he have hated doing it? How could he have spent four years making something so amazing and not enjoyed it?

It makes me wonder. . .

What if he had followed his "North Star" and not done the thing he hated?

I cringe at the thought.

And then I wonder...

What might he have created (and loved creating) in those four years instead?

Or was the Sistine Chapel his North Star and he just didn't realize it at the time?

I don't have the answers.

But it does make me think about my own life, and if I have a small version of my own Sistine Chapel that I might hate doing but that I am meant to do because of all the joy and inspiration it might give to others.

Did Michelangelo love it when it was done? Was it worth it to him?

I know it was to me.

Sometimes Your Worst Is Good Enough

I led a seminar once, long ago. I haven't spoken of it since. It sucked.

Cringe-worthy.

Really.

I am embarrassed even now when I think about it.

Here is some of what one of the participants wrote me afterward:

> Your seminar changed my life. I have never been kind to myself. I have never listened to my own body. I have never given anything to myself. When you told me I was worth it, I teared up. I think you are right. Thank you.

Sometimes it's not about how we perform.

Sometimes just showing up for someone else is good enough.

I would do it again, the exact same way, just for that.

Suck at it!

You never know who might benefit...

Create Thought

What does it mean to create thought? I mean consciously. We all create thought all day long, inadvertently. But what does it mean to consciously create the thoughts we think?

Create: make or cause to be or to become

Thought: to form or have in the mind

How many of us create the form we have in our minds? How old is our programming? Who was the programmer? Who is in charge of your mind today?

Creating thought *is active*, not passive.

Creating thought *is responsible*.

Creating thought *is important*.

Creating thought *is directive*.

Creating our thoughts *brings us our results*.

Creating our thoughts *eliminates blame*.

Creating our thoughts *requires us to tap our creativity*.

Our Creator?

Ourselves.

Are you creating your thoughts? Or, are your thoughts creating you?

Be Fun

The holidays are coming up!

Instead of trying to "have" fun, focus on "being" fun.

I am going to go to a party and *be* fun.

I am going to make Thanksgiving dinner and be the most fun I have ever been. I am going to be so much fun when I hang out with my kids.

Take responsibility for what you bring to each moment.

Be the fun you have.

What Does Peace Feel Like?

I ran across a children's book with this title yesterday while Christmas shopping: *What does peace feel like?*

I bought it.

The book is filled with children's answers to this question.

To me, peace is knowing that everything on the planet and in my day is just as it should be. Even the "bad" stuff was meant to happen...because it did happen. If it wasn't meant to happen, it wouldn't have. The feeling I get, when I believe and know this, is peace. Peace knows it can't change the past.

Peace feels like oxygen in my body. It feels like a deep breath. It feels like relaxing into a comfortable couch. Peace feels like a tingling in my arms. Peace feels like lightness in my belly. Peace feels like there is more to me than this body; it feels expansive and connected and wonderful.

Peace is what happens when we realize that there is nothing worth fighting for that robs us of peace. We don't fight for peace. We stop fighting and then we have peace.

We stop the fighting in our minds first. When we have that peace within our minds, then we can manifest it in our lives.

What does peace feel like to you?

Giving People Permission to Judge You

If you can allow for others to have judgments of you with no resistance back, you will taste a freedom most people will never experience. Other people's judgments are about other people. Their opinions tell us about them, not you.

Byron Katie taught me that pretty much any judgment anyone makes about me is somewhat true. I can usually find where they are right and be okay with it. It doesn't mean there is something wrong with me or that I need to change. It just means that I am human. Human beings are a wonderful mixture of qualities, some good and some bad, depending on who is doing the judging.

I have learned to give people the space they need to judge me, to doubt me, to criticize me, to dislike me, to fight against me, to ridicule me, to complain about me, to mock me, and to disagree with me. I don't have to fight against it or talk to them about it or make a case for myself. I can just be in the allowing of it, which feels so much better.

When the holidays come closer, I have many opportunities to practice this new-found skill. It seems that family members judge each other the most. I find myself doing it. I feel somewhat entitled to judge my sister and brother and mother. Why is that? Because I love them more? Because I have known them longer? I am not sure why — but I do know it feels crappy when I do it. Even so, I give myself and my brain the freedom to judge them. I act like the Watcher. I notice how I feel when I think the judgmental thoughts. I notice how I feel when I don't.

This helps me immensely when I hear them judging me. I know from their place of judgment, they don't feel good. I know from their place of judgment, they are missing out on the connection that is so wonderful to feel. I know their judgment has nothing to do with me, and yet I allow the room for it. I agree with it when I can see where it is true. This allowance, I have noticed, dissolves it. It takes any fuel it has and extinguishes it.

And from there, we can get to the good stuff that lies beyond the judgment. The connection that makes us ALL family beyond any judgment our minds can think up.

Inspired

You guys keep asking me how I feel about the election results.

I received an email from one of my colleagues who is doing a project titled: One Reaction. She wanted to know my "one reaction" to the election.

Here was my reply to her:

INSPIRED.

A young black man got elected to be President of the United States.

What else can this man do?

What can I do?

You?

Today. Is a good day.

Friends as Thought Creators

When we are upset, why do we call a friend? I thought about this yesterday when a friend called me to tell me how upset she was. After we talked for about twenty minutes (not coaching, just chatting) she told me she felt so much better. I hung up the phone and thought about why.

I know I don't have the power to make her feel better, so why did she, in fact, feel better? What was it about our conversation that changed her feelings? Then it occurred to me: *I had given her new thoughts to think.*

I had created better feeling thoughts and passed them over to her like a tray of appetizers. She came to the conversation with these thoughts:

I am so dumb. I can't figure this out. I don't know if I should trust her. I can't do this alone.

I gave her these thoughts to consider, just by saying them out loud:

You are crazy smart. You can totally figure this out. You don't have to work with her if you don't want to. You can do this alone, but you don't have to.

I wasn't even meaning to help her change her thinking, I was just calling it like I see it. But I believe somewhere in that conversation she listened to what I was saying and decided to try one of those thoughts out. As she thought the new thoughts, she felt better. What's even cooler is that I gave her instant evidence that the new thought was true by showing her my conviction in the statement.

Amazing! This is why we love our friends so much. They give us thoughts that make us feel good, and they believe them, which makes it easier for us to believe them ourselves.

So, next time you need a friend and she isn't available, think about what she might say to you. Write it down even. Then try the thoughts out and see how they feel. It will never replace hearing them directly from her, but it might tide you over until you can get her on the phone.

Managing Disappointment

I don't like feeling the emotion of disappointment. It sucks.

I had to do a self-coaching model (ok *five* self-coaching models if you have to know the truth) on my feeling of disappointment over the last few weeks. I have really been diving into this feeling and getting to know what it is all about. Here is what I have come up with:

Disappointment feels heavy, devoid of air, limp. My body slumps when I feel it. I experience lethargy and a mild ache in my body when I am feeling it.

Every thought I questioned that was causing disappointment came from a previous expectation I had created about someone or something. For example, I wanted someone to behave in a certain way and they didn't. I wanted something to play out differently and it didn't. This is me when I try to control my circumstances. Instead of managing my thoughts, I get impossible ideas about controlling the circumstances of my future.

I don't do this by thinking thoughts that are empowering and exciting; I do this by setting myself up as a dependent.

I create a story in my mind about how I can only feel good if the future plays out the way I want it to in specific detail. I don't trust the universe to bring me exactly what I need and accept it when it comes by thinking thoughts that feel good. I push against it and think it shouldn't be happening and then I feel, well, disappointed.

And after spending hours and sometimes days feeling disappointed that it didn't go according to my plan, I see the beauty in the Universal Plan. I see that it went just the way it needed to for my higher good. I see that it is even better than what I could have imagined.

The opposite of disappointment, for me, is gratitude. I am learning (albeit slowly) that I can choose to be thankful for every circumstance I can't control. Gratitude feels light and wonderful! Gratitude kicks disappointment's ass each and every time. Gratitude is a choice.

The thought that I plug into the self coaching model for gratitude is this:

Thought: *I know I can access the intelligence within me to show me how this is the perfect circumstance for me right now.*

Feeling: *Gratitude*

Action: *Do the self work required and move onto the next thing.*

Result: *Peaceful coexistence with my circumstances and amazing access to ideas.*

Try this next time you feel disappointed and you won't be.

I Don't Like Her

Think about how this statement makes you feel. Suspend your judgment of her (or him) for a minute and think about what this thought causes you to feel. Check in with your body.

Not so good, right?

I know that you think it is *her* you don't like, but really it is your THOUGHTS about her that you don't like.

When a client says to me that they don't like someone, I correct them and tell them that it is more accurate to say they don't like their *thoughts* about them. This inevitably starts an argument. (My favorite.) The client wants to go on and on about the person's behavior, things they say, wear, or even how they smell. I always bring them back to the reality that none of that can affect them in any way if they don't have a thought about it.

Right now think about someone you think you don't like. What are your thoughts about this person? Isn't it true that it's your thoughts about them you don't like? Is it just as easy to think better feeling thoughts about the person? Not for their sake, but for yours?

What does it feel like when you think, *"I do like her."* Notice how that thought feels in your body.

Better, right?

Isn't that good to know?

I also know that I prefer to like people rather than not like them.

I have stopped saying, "I don't like people," because one day I noticed it didn't feel good to think that thought.

I now say, "I like her; I just prefer not to spend time with her."

Feels way better to me. Try it out.

Think thoughts that feel good.

I like you when you do that.

Balance

I can't stand it when coaches use this word. Every time I hear it I cringe, even if I am the one saying it.

I don't believe in balance. I don't want balance.

I love extremes.

But only if they're fun.

Seriously, how many times have you beaten yourself up because you aren't balanced enough? Maybe you don't spend enough time with the kids or cook sit down meals or balance your checkbook or call your mother enough. You think if you had more balance in your life you would do all of these things. Everything would have its special place in the balance pie.

To me, balance means you do everything a little and you don't really get knee deep in any of it.

This last weekend I went on vacation with my best friend. There was nothing balanced about it. We water skied until we couldn't move our bodies, we ate licorice for breakfast, we laughed until our husbands rolled their eyes and we plotted how to do it all again next week.

We are both full time mothers and full time workers. We don't balance.

Sometimes we forget to feed our kids. ("Goodnight, Mom. I love you. Why didn't we eat dinner today?") Sometimes we forget to do our work because we are playing with our kids. And sometimes we just spend three hours getting pedicures on Tuesday when the house is a mess and there is a pile of work to do on our desks. Balance wouldn't allow for any of this fun.

My mom raised me to be well-rounded. She wanted me to be good at most things and have lots of experiences but I think I turned out very pointy and extreme. I don't want a good income; I want to be a multi-millionaire. I don't want to be a good coach; I want to rock my clients' worlds. I don't want work-life balance; I want a complete over-lapped mess. I want to accept that I forgot to feed my kids on Wednesday, but then made a four-course meal on Thursday.

I am tired of beating myself up for what I am not, and I am tired of hearing my friends do the same. I want to be who I am, outright extreme and intense and joy-chasing. I want my kids to see that and not "balance." I am going to step off the tight-rope of perfection so balance isn't re-quired and live my life from one extreme to another.

Wanna join me?

Every Victim Needs a Villain

Do you have a villain in your life?

Maybe it's your mother. Maybe it's your father. Maybe it's the neighbor who abused you or the kid in school who bullied you. Maybe it is your boss or your mother-in-law. Maybe it's your spouse.

I am always fascinated when I hear people talk about their villains. They do it so matter-of-factly. They blame and judge and bash their villains. They talk about them in truly hateful ways.

I know someone — let's call her Sophia — who lives with this villain mentality. She refers to her villain often. She talks about how much her villain is materialistic, how selfish she is, what a bitch she is, how uncaring she has been to her, how self-absorbed she is, how mean she is. She talks to her friends and family about her villain and how she has shaped and caused so much pain in her life.

The title of her story is: "If Only My Villain Had Been Nicer."

I am so bored with her painful sob story that I could stab myself with a pencil, seriously. I try to understand why she must go on and on with the undercurrent of judgment. I have tried to join her in her judgment and found myself just feeling like crap. I have tried to talk to her about her judgment, and she is so emphatic that we get nowhere. I have tried to listen and understand, but frankly I just don't.

Then, today, as I am driving in my car it occurs to me. She has a victim mentality. She sees herself as a victim. Holy crap! This is not a person I had ever seen this way but, truth be told, this fact hit me like a ton of bricks. She holds on so tightly to her story because of her need to define herself as the victim in her life.

Wow, that sucks. She isn't my client so I can't call her up and let her know about my profound insight, and yet it comforts me to understand it more. I get now why she needs to reinforce and repeat the perpetrator story for her own self-definition. I can be more relaxed now when she goes into her hateful, blaming barrage.

It's just her thoughts about her being a victim projected onto her chosen perpetrator.

Then I wonder......do I have a villain? I know I used to. It used to be my dad, then it was my mom, then it was my boss......but now, as I think about it, I realize I don't have a villain. I don't blame anyone for anything in my life. Honestly. I see now that everything that has happened has been for my ultimate good. I don't argue with my past or my reality.

I have no need for a villain in my life because I am very clear: I am not a victim.

Astounding.

Do you have a villain?

I Am Not _____ Enough

I was working with one of my clients this week who was convinced she wasn't smart enough. I spent most of the session laughing at her so-called proof for this limiting belief. (It's my latest tool — Belief Mockery.) It went something like this:

I know I graduated college with a high GPA without studying, but that doesn't mean I am smart.

I know that I got a very high score on the GRE with very little studying, but that doesn't really mean I am smart.

I know that I was one of six accepted into an MA program, but that is beside the point.

I know that I found it very easy to get a masters degree while others struggled, but it was so easy for me that it doesn't really count.

This is the point where you can insert me laughing hysterically. She is crying because she takes this story very seriously, but I am laughing at how ridiculous her logic has become in order to hang onto this limitation.

So I asked her how she defined the word "smart."

She said, "Well, you are very smart."

(Insert much more Brooke laughter here.)

I asked again, "How do you define smart?"

She answered with, "The ability to retain and recall information."

I reminded her that I don't know where Iowa is on the map and I have to use spell checker to spell the word, "response."

She said, "Who cares about that? You are such a smart coach and you know exactly what to say to coach your clients."

"Yes," I said, "I am smart in exactly the ways I need to be smart and not smart in others. I am exactly smart enough. I don't need to be smart in grammar because I am not meant to be an editor. I need to be smart in coaching because that is my destiny."

She got it. She agreed. She was so relieved.

She said, "I am exactly as smart as I need to be to fulfill my destiny."

Yes she is. So are you.

You are exactly as smart as you need to be.

You are exactly as thin as you need to be.

You are exactly as loved as you need to be.

You are exactly as pretty, knowledgeable, organized, social, athletic, and brilliant in the areas you need to be to fulfill your destiny.

That's why it's easy — you're meant to do it.

So fill in the blank for yourself:

I am exactly as _____ as I need to be.

What Do You Think about You?

We spend so much time thinking about this.

I mean really think about this. That question, "Does my butt look big?" isn't about you; it is about the people behind you. It is about others.

What about the way you decorate your house? The car you drive? A title on your business card? How much of that is about you and your relationship with yourself? How much of it is how you want others to perceive of you and think of you?

So many times in a session a client will say to me something like, "I don't want you to think I am dumb," when they are telling me about their thoughts or actions. They will say, "I have gotten so much better, you should have seen me last year." Other similar things you might say or think might include:

I don't want to hurt her feelings. I don't want him to feel bad. I don't want them to hate me. I want them to validate me. I don't want to seem like a bitch to them.

The bummer about this type of thinking is that we can't control what others think or feel. Ever. They get to decide what they want to think about you, with or without your input. They have their opinion and they have control of their opinion.

You may go out of your way to act nice in order for them to think you are nice. You may act intelligent or sincere or sophisticated in order for them to think that you are these things even when they are not what you are feeling in the moment.

This is so much wasted energy.

This is you pretending.

It's exhausting.

And it never ends.

Trying to control other people and what they think is impossible. We can barely control what we think, how do we expect to control what others think?

And even if you could control what others think by how you behave, what does that really do for you? What does it buy you? A full-time job of acting in a way that controls how they think so you can feel good.

That's the long, tiring way around.

If you want to feel good all you have to do is control your own thinking. That is a big enough job. Other people's thoughts are about other people.

Your thoughts about you are what matter.

What do you think about you?

Don't Mistake Indulgence for Abundance

Abundance comes from within us.

Indulgence comes from without.

Indulgence is put upon us.
Dessert, sauces, alcohol,
comfort, service, luxury,
expensive clothes, jewels, spa treatments.

Abundance is.

It's Being.

It isn't found in things.
It isn't found at all.

It emerges when unencumbered.
It flows.

It illuminates.

It attracts
never-ending abundance.

It never worries about not being enough.

Being is always enough.

It isn't stuffed, encouraged, managed or stressed.

It's free from worry, which pretends to be important.

Free from....too much.

Free from indulgence.

Abundance.

Wanting

There are two ways to want. You can want from a place of believing or you can want from a place of doubt. The only difference is pain.

When you want something (like thinness), and you believe you will have it, you most likely will feel excited and happy and motivated. I remember the moment when this happened to me. I had committed to taking better care of myself and had been at it for a while when it occurred to me that I would be thin and I would never abuse my body again. It was exhilarating. I was still in my heavier body, but I was bouncing around with excitement. I was happy; I wanted more, and I believed I would get it.

Most often, new clients come to me and want with doubt. They want to be thin more than almost anything, and they are very doubtful that this will ever happen for them. Even though they have hired me with mild hope that "this" will work, deep down they later admit that they don't believe it will.

I think this is why many people just stop wanting. "I want for nothing," they will say. "I have just accepted that I will be obese and that this is just my life." It is heartbreaking and completely unnecessary. I do think it is important to keep wanting. Wanting more is how we grow and how we are inspired to action. I think what we want is actually very important information, that when followed can lead us to the life we are most joyful living.

So think about what you want in your life and notice how it feels to want it. If it feels good, you most likely believe that you will have it. If it feels painful, there may be some doubtful thoughts that you can work through in order to unleash your inspiration to act.

You can follow these steps:

1. Write down what you want.

2. Write down the feeling associated with the want.

3. If it feels painful, write down why you believe you might not have what you want.

4. Evaluate these thoughts of doubt for logic and then test their turnarounds.

5. Change these thoughts to thoughts that support your belief that you can and will have what you want.

6. Repeat as necessary.

What I want is for you to live in your body at its natural weight and to eat in a way that feels healthy and invigorating to you. I am feeling very good about this want because I believe you can and will have it!

Being Myself

In my practice, my main goal with my clients is to show them that they are spectacular. No matter what they think about themselves or accept about themselves, I encourage them to at least BE themselves.

In almost any situation a client can ask me what to do and I can answer with "Be yourself. Tell the truth. The people who accept your truth are your people. The people who don't accept your truth aren't your people and that is OK."

I know this is easier than it sounds. I live my truth. I tell my truth. And, frankly, some people don't like it and some people do. But that is not relevant. I believe that I am meant to live in an authentic and genuine way, and sometimes that is just plain confusing.

For example: I LOVE the work of Byron Katie and Abraham. I love to meditate. I love yoga. I can sit in silence for hours and not get bored. I love hiking in silence. BUT I also love Dane Cook and loud '80s rap. I love obnoxious laughter and having so much fun I get kicked out of a restaurant.

I love kindness — that deep, unabashed, loving, unconditional, I-would-do-anything-for-you kindness. But I also love sarcasm and mockery. I love expensive cars like BMWs and Mercedes, but I also love Velveeta Cheese and plastic plates from Walmart.

I love technology and email and iPhones, but I also love nature and wild animals and our planet. I am loud and in-your-face and bold, and then sometimes I am quiet and very shy.

I eat high-grade fuel for my body and then every once in a while I order and eat nachos from Taco Bell.

I am a mass of contradictions. I am confusing and unpredictable. It is exciting and fun and scary and humbling living this life in a way that feels authentic.

I have friends who cringe when I swear and others who complain when I don't. I have friends who are atheists and friends who are Catholics. I love them all deeply. I notice they have contradictions just like me. I notice they are as confused by themselves and by this life just as much as I am.

But what I also notice is that when I live my life in a way that feels "Brooke," in a way that feels authentically true, I am happy. It doesn't mean I won't change my mind or switch directions or live in complete contradiction. It just means that I seek my truth and live it no matter what. And the people who can stand it will stay and those who can't will leave, and I can't blame them. But I always have me. And that is enough.

Are you living your truth?

I Am Not Your Magic

I am not your magic.

I am *my* magic.

And you are yours.

You First!

Many of you have heard me talk about this before but too bad. I have had to coach this so much lately that I wanted to give us all a reminder.

What is it you think THEY aren't doing or should be doing? Come on. Think about it. Here are a few I have heard in the last three days:

He should respect me.
She should not copy me.
They should be nicer to me.
He should compliment me.
He should notice my body.
He should acknowledge I have lost weight.
He should take me to nice dinners.
She should listen to me.
She could care more.
She acts like I don't exist.

Honestly, what we expect from THEM!!! They should be able to do it all the time for us. No matter that we can't muster a kind word for ourselves ever, and we can't re-member the last time we gave ourselves a compliment! But *they* better damn well do it.

When I tell my client to be more kind to herself, she tells me it is too difficult. She tells me that it is hard to remember. She tells me that she forgets.

SHE CAN'T DO IT FOR HERSELF AND YET IS PISSED THAT HER BOYFRIEND WON'T DO IT.

When I tell my client to pay attention to herself when she feels like her daughter doesn't return her phone calls, she tells me she doesn't know how.

BUT SHE EXPECTS HER DAUGHTER TO KNOW HOW.

I want my husband to stop getting frustrated at me when I forget things. I want him to be more patient and understanding.

AND YET I CAN'T CUT MYSELF ANY SLACK SOMETIMES.

So notice, my friends, the next time you want something from someone, my guess is you aren't giving it to yourself.

Marianne Williamson taught me that *A Course in Miracles* says: "The only thing missing in any situation is what you aren't giving."

You want more love. Love yourself. You want more attention.

HELLO SELF.

You want kindness. When is the last time you were truly kind and loving to you?

Confusion vs. Commitment

I have a client right now who has been at this a while and is very tuned into herself. She recently sent me an email about how confused she was. She talked about how she couldn't decide what to do or when to do it. And even when she did make a decision, she second guessed herself and then was confused again. She, very brilliantly, came to the conclusion that she must "get" something from being confused because she did it often. Being confused is a choice that she recognized she was making.

I replied to her and told her that I thought confusion is a way of staying out of the game. It is a way of not committing. It's a way of being on the sidelines. Confused people aren't in the moment and they rarely take connected and inspired action, they just sit in unproductive rumination.

After reading her email, I realized that many of my clients and readers are in this same place. Many of you are confused.

"Will this program work for me? "What am I supposed to eat?" "How much should I exercise?" "Should I even bother losing weight?" "I don't think I understand how to feel my feelings."

These are statements I hear over and over from confused readers who genuinely want to lose weight. Confusion is getting in the way. Confusion is keeping them from taking action.

So, from now on, choose clarity. It really is as easy as making a decision. The statements would look more like this: "This program is going to work for me." "I know exactly what my body needs." "I know how to feel." "I will lose this weight." These are the beliefs and statements that define a commitment to yourself and your process by saying, "I am not sure what to do," you lie to yourself and keep yourself from committing to your dreams.

The worst thing that can happen if you make a choice to believe in yourself is that you have made a choice to believe in yourself. You have chosen commitment over confusion. It truly is a choice. Make it!

Nancy Doesn't Want To Eat

Nancy is my mother-in-law. She has cancer.

We went to visit her the other day and there was a tray of food untouched by her bed. There was a piece of decadent chocolate cake on her night stand. I asked her about it. She made a blah face at me and said, "Doesn't taste good."

Nancy used to love food. She used to make German chocolate cake and fight my husband for the crumbs. She used to worry about her weight. She used to cook and eat a lot. She always looked robust and healthy. She was always trying to lose weight.

And now she has. She has lost forty pounds. The scale reads 115. One fifteen was her goal weight. The scale doesn't know she has cancer.

Tell Your Truth

Recently, I was struggling with what to do in a highly tense situation. There were many people involved and some of them were having conflict. I didn't want to hurt anyone's feelings or make the conflict worse by making the "wrong" decision. I struggled and struggled in my mind asking myself, "Which course of action would be most helpful and benign to the conflict?"

When I couldn't come up with the right answer, I asked one of the people involved what she thought I should do. She looked at me without hesitation and with no agenda and said, "I think you should do what you want to do."

It was amazing. Such a simple solution!

So I went inside myself and ignored the conflict and the people involved and asked myself what I wanted. Immediately the answer was completely clear and the struggle within me dissolved. Literally it took one minute from the time I asked the question.

Later that same day this same person was struggling with her own decision concerning the conflict. As we were talking it became clear she wasn't sure how to communicate with the person she was having a conflict with. She was trying to come up with the right words and the right behavior in order not to hurt this person's feelings and yet still get what she needed. Here is what I said to her: "Tell him the truth. Straight up."

I believe that we need to tell our truth, and when we do people will react.

The people who react with judgment and anger are not our people.

She agreed.

So what amazes me about this whole experience is that we both took seemingly very complex and tense situations and made them simple and clear in a very short period of time by asking ourselves what our own truth was. By asking:

What do I want?
What is my truth?

We eliminated the confusion and found relief immediately. By eliminating conflict and confusion, we eliminate many of the feelings that lead to fog eating. By remaining clear in our minds, we can remain clear in our eating. Not sure what to do?

Ask yourself for the truth.

Never Settle

Think about all the areas of your life and in which areas you know deep down inside you are settling when you deserve better. For some of you it is your job, for others it is the state of your relationships. For most of you, it is your body and health. In these areas you know you want more, but you have accepted bad or good instead of great. In Jim Collins' book, *Good to Great* he explains that good is the enemy of great. I love this idea. It is the recipe for a mediocre life, when you know you could have a fantastic one.

My longest, dearest friend recently realized this about her life. She looked up from her daily routine of work, kids, husband, house, and body and realized she was settling. She was going through her days on automatic pilot with "no complaints." She knew that things weren't as good as they could be, but she had settled for "good enough." So she decided to do something about it. She decided that if she wasn't moving forward toward the life she wanted, she was moving away from it. She learned the lesson that there is no standing still. You are either actively creating the life you want or you are taking what you "get." She started connecting with her body and doing her emotional work and lost twenty pounds in a few months. She started looking for a new job, found one and gave notice to her current employer. To her surprise, her current employer came to her and offered her to name her price in order to keep her at the company. She is now doing the same job for almost twice the amount of money! And finally, she decided to more actively engage in her relationship with her husband to make it better than just good and it became full of compliments, not just absent of complaints.

I saw her in person recently and she was glowing. She was alive and awake in her own life. She seemed proud and full of self-respect. She wasn't settling. She was moving forward into the life she wants and deserves.

What are you settling for in your life? What do you want to move toward instead?

But I Deserve It!

"I deserved to eat it." I have heard this reason for overeating more times than I can count. Clients will eat at a meal even when they aren't hungry, they will eat dessert when they are already at full, or they will eat at a party after a long week all in the name of "deserving it."

But let me tell you what you are really saying when you say you deserve food you don't want or need:

I deserve to be uncomfortable.
I deserve to feel guilty.
I deserve to jeopardize my health.
I deserve to be disconnected from my body.
I deserve to not really enjoy or taste my food.
I deserve to live heavier than my natural weight.
I deserve to struggle.

You do not deserve any of the above. It is punishing and unkind. Eating past fullness or when you aren't joy-eating is like turning your back on yourself and looking over your shoulder at yourself and saying, "Too bad, you deserve this."

YOU DON'T DESERVE PUNISHMENT.

Whatever messed up belief you have pulled from your childhood that you blame yourself for has no relevance in your life now. Punishing yourself for something you THINK you did in your past is useless.

Here is what you deserve no matter what you think you have done:

You deserve to be happy.

You deserve to stop eating when your body doesn't need more fuel.

You deserve to enjoy each bite of a joy food.

You deserve to say "no" to food when you aren't hungry.

You deserve your own love.

You deserve your own protection.

You deserve kind thoughts toward yourself.

You deserve to live in a healthy, strong and lean body.

You deserve the feeling of lightness and freedom.

So please don't eat some chocolate concoction in the name of "deserving it."

You deserve better.

I Don't Have to Worry about My Weight

Neither do you.

Worrying about anything is a choice.

As many of you know, I am a Law of Attraction freak. I think Esther, Jerry and Abraham rock. Everything I read of theirs resonates with me on the deepest of levels. It complements the work I have been doing with my clients for years.

The basic premise/truth that I teach my clients is this: Your THOUGHTS create your FEELINGS — which create your ACTIONS — which create your RESULTS. Your results will always prove the original thought, whether you like it or not. So basically, if you believe that you will always be fat, you will feel fat, you will eat too much, and then you will gain weight proving your original thought.

The Law of Attraction says the same thing but uses different words. It states: Your FOCUS creates your VIBRATION — which is what MANIFESTS — which attracts more of what you are focused on. Same truth. Different words.

So, going back to worrying about your weight, the FEELING is worry. I teach my clients to find the feeling and feel it. Then, I suggest they find the thought causing it. (Remember all feelings are caused by thoughts.) In this case the thought may be: "I will never lose this weight and my health will suffer." (You may think this is a fact, but really it is just your thought.) The good news is that if you want to stop the feeling of worry, all you have to do is change the thought.

Easy, right?

Well, this is where the Law of Attraction may help me explain. The Law of Attraction basically states that we attract to us what we are vibrating outwardly. And if we stay with the idea that feelings are really the vibrations in our body, then you can imagine what the vibration of "worry" might attract. More worry. More things to worry about. Because, as Abraham would say, "When you push against what you don't want, you are giving it your attention and attracting it."

So worry is focusing on the worst. Worrying is actually thinking about what you don't want. If you are worried it is because you have a belief or a thought that is not serving you.

Okay, so what should you do?

It is actually quite simple. Focus on changing your thoughts. Unwind the crappy ones and think about what you genuinely want. You will know when you have a great thought because it will make you FEEL amazing to think it. The more you think about it, the better you will feel and the more of it you will attract into your life.

If you find yourself thinking the thought and you feel icky, it is because you are thinking about not having it. Reword the thought so when you focus on it, you imagine yourself having it and feeling amazing having it.

The thoughts and the feelings come first. Remember, you may think you want the result (thinness) so you can stop worrying about your weight. But the truth is, you have to change your thoughts to stop worrying so you can take inspired action, manifest, or attract the result.

If you feel good, you are doing it perfectly!

Prove Yourself Wrong

I have heard the negative beliefs over and over. They are all some version of the following belief:

"I can't lose weight; there is something wrong with me."

I have also heard all the proof for this belief. It includes past attempts and diets, no motivation to exercise, slow metabolism, no willpower and genetics. This "evidence" is spoken to me as irrefutable truth. The broken self-promises are all pulled out as proof that you are somehow broken and not able to lose weight permanently without a struggle.

I am here to tell you that you are WRONG.

I know that sometimes it is hard to hear that everything you have believed for so many years is a lie, but it is. I know that you might have been told that you have to go on some crazy diet or get surgery in order to keep weight off permanently. I know that there are many examples of other people who have attempted to lose weight and have been unsuccessful. But none of this is evidence that proves you cannot accomplish permanent weight loss for yourself.

You can lose weight, keep it off, and end the struggle.

Period.

I don't care what anyone else has told you. I don't care how heavy your mother is. I don't care how your sister struggles too. None of that means you can't be free from overeating and excess weight.

So I am asking you to prove yourself wrong. Be willing to admit that you have made a huge mistake in believing that you can't lose weight. You have really screwed up in perpetuating the struggle by believing that somehow you don't have what it takes to live in a body that is at a comfortable and at a natural weight.

It was hard for me to admit that I was wrong. I don't like being wrong (just ask my husband). But I was wrong. There wasn't something different about me that made it impossible to lose weight. I was wrong when I believed my mother when she told me, "You will always be a big girl, and you will always have to watch your weight." She was wrong and I was wrong to believe her.

I am tall — not big. And I don't have to watch my weight; I have to watch my beliefs. And when I find one that is not serving me or working for me, I am willing to prove myself wrong.

Are you willing to prove yourself wrong?

Happiness Is the Consequence of Personal Effort

"Happiness is the consequence of personal effort"
~Liz Gilbert

Notice that Liz, author of *Eat, Pray, Love,* does not say that happiness is the result of personal punishment. She doesn't say that if you beat yourself up enough and starve yourself enough and then work out hard enough so you can barely stand enough that you will be happy. She says that you make an effort to be happy.

So many of my clients tell me they will be happy after they beat themselves into submission with a rigorous diet. They say they will be happy when they are thin. They say they will be happy when their career takes off. But happiness is something you can create or access. Being kind to yourself and having compassion for yourself can connect you to yourself and the happiness that is already residing within you.

You cannot go on a path of self-criticism and expect to find joy at the end. The path of self-criticism and self-punishment leads to pain. Always has.

It Takes Energy

It takes energy to gain weight.

It takes energy to go into debt.

It takes energy to be angry at someone you love.

Overeating.

Overspending.

Judging.

It all takes energy.

If you do nothing, you can't be in debt. Going into debt takes way more energy than staring at a wall. Debt doesn't just happen to you. You don't wake up one day in debt.

You have to apply and get a credit card.

You have to activate it.

You have to buy something with it.

You have to pay the bill (or the minimum payment).

You have to apply and get a second credit card.

That is how debt "happens."

You use your precious, limited life-supply of energy to go into debt.

And then you spend more energy suffering the debt.

More energy complaining about the debt.

More of your energy getting out of debt.

Same with getting overweight.

Same with fighting.

It would be easier and take much less effort to do nothing.

In fact, doing nothing just might be a fabulous idea to consider.

Who's Controlling You?

I have a most beautiful client who has the most heinous sister.

Just ask her.

She said she wanted to have nothing to do with her sister, and was very upset that her sister pissed her off so much.

So, I asked her if she would rather like her sister or not like her sister.

She said if those were the only two choices she would rather like her.

(Now, I realize that in her mind she is imagining liking a better-behaved sister.)

I told her that I had some great news for her.

I told her that her sister was not making her mad.

I told her that her thoughts were.

Then I asked her who she thought *felt* the "dislike" when she disliked her sister.

She said her sister.

But then I asked it again. Who feels YOUR dislike for your sister? Who feels that emotion?

Then she realized it was she who felt the dislike. It was she who felt that negativity within her body.

I explained to her that I thought the reason she said she would rather like her sister was for her own sake because it FEELS better to like than to dislike someone.

And then I told her that she was giving her sister the power to determine how she feels.

Her sister, with her behavior, was sending her an invitation to feel bad and she was accepting with gusto. Every time her sister behaved in a way that she thought was unreasonable, she felt anger and dislike.

Her sister's behavior dictated her emotions in that moment.

She asked me how to change that. (She obviously did not like the idea of her sister determining anything for her.)

I told her that she could acknowledge that the truth is her sister cannot determine how she feels without her consent. She could take a look at the thoughts causing her to feel dislike and anger and find a thought that was more neutral for her.

I did not ask her to go from disliking her sister to loving her sister.

I asked her to try to go from disliking her sister to feeling neutral about her sister. To do this for her own sake, so she didn't have to feel the unpleasant feeling of disliking someone.

She did.

Her thought changed from: *"My sister is unreasonable."*

To: *"My sister doing what my sister does."*

She felt relief.

Isn't it amazing how we do this to ourselves? We cause ourselves to feel negative emotions, and we give our emotional control away to someone we claim not to like.

I do it often myself.

Not a good plan.

I try to remember that I get to decide how to feel, no matter how anyone acts towards me.

That, my friends, is freedom.

Be Willing to Be Destroyed

Many of my clients are afraid to feel. They think once they open the door they will be overcome with so much pain and darkness, they will slip into a depression never to be heard from again.

They eat mountains of food to avoid this destruction. They stay in the wrong relationship, the wrong job, the wrong body, and the wrong city all to avoid being destroyed emotionally.

And in this resistance to destruction, they create a long, slow erosion of their authentic selves.

They create the destruction.

I have been destroyed many times in my life.

I'm not going to lie. It sucks. Bad.

But once the dust settles, I can begin again. I can let go of the parts of me that needed to be obliterated. My fear. My doubt. My shame. My fear. My fear. My fear.

Because there is something enlightening about letting or making the worst thing that can happen, happen.

It's over. It's done. It's destroyed.

Emotionally raw, with no defenses. We are left without fear of pain.

And in its place?

Hope.

Three Things to Do with a Negative Feeling

Step 1: Avoid it

Step 2: Feel it

Step 3: Use it

We **avoid** our feelings by consulpting. (Consuming something compulsively.) This always just adds a layer of ick to the negative feeling we already have. We feel lonely. We avoid it with three bowls of Lucky Charms. We feel full instead.

We **feel** our feelings by naming them. Noticing them in our bodies. Paying attention. We listen for the thoughts causing the feelings and write them down. We stay connected even when it feels bad.

We **use** our feelings when we find the thoughts causing them and do the thought work to change them. Then, by harnessing the energy of the emotion (and there is a lot of energy there to use), we can use it to create the life of our dreams perhaps using the energy of anger to train for a marathon or the energy of lonely to compose a song.

If you notice you are still avoiding yourself by avoiding your feelings, don't worry about it. You are just in step one. When you get to step three, the problem you had is now your fuel for the solution

Use it.

Other People's Brilliance

OK. Now this is important. When you look at other people's brilliant work, how do you feel?

Jealous?

Inadequate?

Shocked they're so successful because you know you could do better?

Or inspired?

I read Geneen Roth and want to weep with how amazingly she composes a book. She inspires me to create something beautiful.

Hugh MacLeod, ignoring everyone all the way to the bank, makes me want to stand on my couch and high-five the air.

My husband's kindness, when he picks up garbage at a public park, makes me want to feed starving children all over the world.

Feeling diminished by someone's success or good fortune is wasting an opportunity to be inspired.

Other people's brilliant lives bring more brilliance to the world, not less.

And I, for one, am thankful and better for it.

Creating Emotion

Creating your own emotion deliberately does not mean you don't feel emotions.

It doesn't mean you pretend you're not feeling negative emotion.

Just the opposite.

You acknowledge the negative emotion, find its cause and then you create an alternative.

It means being able to create the emotion you want to feel with your thinking, with your mind.

This is important to know how to do.

It is the way to get what you want.

Your emotions are what dictate your actions and your results.

Negative emotions from negative thinking never garner positive results.

That is not how the Law of Attraction works. Ever.

When you use your mind to create emotion, instead of relying on external circumstances to change your thoughts, you find true empowerment. True deliberate creation.

You don't "act" like you feel good, you genuinely create the feel good first and then it comes.

Feeling amazing on purpose and for real is the beginning (not the end) of getting what you want.

What emotion have you created today?

What do you expect tomorrow?

Are they in alignment?

Inspiring vs. Impressing

Which one does your life do?

I used to be all about impressing other people.

Look at me!

Look at my outfit, my car, my cute apartment, my grades.

Look at how much weight I can lose!

But as Martha Beck says, "When people are busy being impressed looking *at* you, they might not ever *see* you."

And they didn't see me.

I didn't even see me.

Even when I was able to impress someone, it didn't give me peace. It gave me the feeling of anxiety because I felt I needed to keep impressing them.

More clothes, more weight to lose, more make-up to buy....

Then I went to a seminar and wrote a mission statement for my life: *I want to be an example of what is possible.*

As I started to live my life based on this new desire, I stopped trying to impress. I started to get to know myself and learn what I truly wanted and what I was capable of doing.

I wanted what was possible for my life. I wanted to show myself what I could be.

It was a good decision.

After losing weight and keeping it off, I became much less interested in showing off and impressing, and much more interested in inspiring others to figure out why they were overeating.

It led to my life of being a coach. Of being seen. And seeing.

What about you?

Are you trying to get people to look at you?

Or are you letting them really see you?

Shhhh. Don't Over-Think It.

Yesterday, my friend Lorie says to me, "Shhhhh. Don't over-think it."

I was going on and on about one of our mutual friend's actions.

Trying to explain why.

Coming up with elaborate theories as to how.

Guessing and alleging...

She just shushed me.

I immediately let it go and felt free.

It was awesome.

I have used it a couple more times today with the same results.

My husband received a tension-filled phone call.

My thoughts went crazy.

I just told them to shhhhhhh. I said, "Don't over-think it," to my mind.

Immediate freedom and relief.

Did the same thing when the kids were being mean to each other.

I told my mind to shhhh.

It worked.

Seriously.

Try it.

What Is Your Mind Set To?

I was listening to Eminem yesterday. In "Lose Yourself," at the end, he says, "You can do anything you set your mind to."

I thought a lot about this.

"Set your mind."

"Mindset."

So, I started to think about what my mind is set to.

I would like to say it's set to happiness.

Like a setting on the oven, I would like to think my setting is perfect for cooking joy and laughter.

Lots of laughing.

To me, I guess my mindset is the "set" of supporting thoughts that give me the result I am looking for.

I am convinced that some of the people I come into contact with have their minds set to complaining.

Or worry. Or failure. Or self-pity.

Why?

The only reason I can think of is that they aren't paying attention. They don't consciously set their minds.

They just "cook" on whatever setting was left yesterday.

Think about it.

What is YOUR mindset?

What result have you set YOUR mind to?

It's Not a Race, and You're the Winner

In one of our coaching calls, Meadow said to a client, "It's not a race, so no one's ahead of you."

Not sure why, but the way she said it on that particular day, knocked the wind out of me.

It's not?

We're not in a race?

Then why are we all running so fast?

Looking over our shoulders?

Checking our watches?

Frantically looking for the finish line?

Why are we freaked out when people are ahead of us?

Someone forgot to tell us that we aren't in a race against each other.

I'm so glad Meadow remembered.

The race is over.

We've already won.

Time to claim our prize.

It's here. Now.

Be Willing to Suck at It

I received an email this week from a client who had ordered my Coach in a Box product. She told me she was getting a lot out of the product, but noticed that in my book and in my workbook I used the wrong tense often and there were too many typos.

After reading this email, I reminded myself that I really have no business being an author. Half the time I don't know where to put a comma, what tense is appropriate and I consistently end sentences in prepositions. The only reason I know about the prepositions is that my mother (who is the one who should be an author) points this out to me regularly. Otherwise I am sure I wouldn't even notice.

I did try to get someone to write the book for me. I really did. I hired a ghostwriter because one of my coaches told me it was very common and "everyone" does it. When I got the first chapters back, the grammar was perfect, but the content was ridiculous. This guy knew about writing, but he didn't know anything about emotional eating. So I had to write the book myself. I did hire an editor, but not even she could catch all the mistakes on the first round. It was that bad.

But here is the thing I was willing to suck at it. When I train new coaches I have to remind them regularly to be willing to be imperfect, be willing to make mistakes, and be willing to do a terrible job. It really is the only way we can improve and get better at anything. I realize this is easier said than done. Putting yourself out there without "being perfect," automatically opens you up to all sorts of constructive and non-constructive criticism. Just reading the reviews on Amazon can send some of my fellow author/coaches into bed for days. It means someone might think less of you or lose respect for you. They may even laugh and make fun of you.

So I could have waited until I learned better grammar to write a book. I could have let the ghostwriter turn out an error-free product. Or I could have obsessed about how I will never in twenty million years write a book as well as Harvard educated Dr. Martha Beck. But I didn't. I sucked at it. And if I hadn't been willing to suck at it, I wouldn't have received this email:

> Brooke,
> A friend gave me your book, If I Am So Smart, Why Can't I
> Lose Weight? Like millions of others, my friend and I have
> wrestled with our weight since childhood. I've always said that
> no one knows more about losing weight than a fat person. I
> am pleased to eat (metaphorically) those words! I've been
> 'moved' by many things, including holding a length of hard-
> ened artery removed from my mother; but nothing has ever
> moved me the way your book has. You put things into a
> perspective I can finally grasp and call my own. I have been
> crying for the past couple of hours. I know I'm crying because I

feel deep hurt at how I've treated me, and I'm crying because
for the first time in my life I feel so much hope I can hardly
handle it. Both reasons are good, and I'm so thankful you had
the experiences you did so you could write this book. There's so
much more I want to say, but don't have the time, as I'm at
work. I keep a journal, and if you don't mind, I'd like to share
my experiences with you from time to time.
God Bless You
Rondi

What gifts are you selfishly hoarding because you aren't
willing to suck at it? Your "Rondi" is waiting.

When Will You Arrive?

When will you arrive?

At a size 6?

At one million dollars?

When Mr. Right marries you?

When you find your purpose?

Maybe when you arrive,

    you will realize

        the trip is over...

CPSIA information can be obtained
at www.ICGtesting.com
Printed in the USA
BVOW06s2309210917
495547BV00017B/117/P